28 YEARS LATER

Also by Alex Garland

screenplays

28 DAYS LATER

SUNSHINE

NEVER LET ME GO

DREDD

EX MACHINA

ANNIHILATION

CIVIL WAR

WARFARE (with Ray Mendoza)

novels

THE BEACH

THE TESSERACT

THE COMA

28 YEARS LATER

screenplay by

ALEX GARLAND

faber

First published in 2025
by Faber & Faber Ltd
The Bindery, 51 Hatton Garden
London EC1N 8HN

First published in the USA in 2025

Typeset by Brighton Gray
Printed in Canada by Marquis Book Printing

A CIP record for this book is available from the British Library

ISBN 978-0-571-39863-8

Printed and bound in Canada on FSC® certified paper in line with our continuing
commitment to ethical business practices, sustainability and the environment.

For further information see faber.co.uk/environmental-policy.

Our authorised representative in the EU for product safety is
Easy Access System Europe, Mustamäe tee 50, 10621 Tallinn, Estonia
gpsr.requests@easproject.com

2 4 6 8 10 9 7 5 3 1

28 YEARS LATER

OPEN ON –

EXT. HOUSE – DAY

– a boy.

His name is JIMMY.

He's ten years old. Striking blond hair. Terrified. Running out of the back door of his house.

As he runs, a necklace with a GOLD CRUCIFIX *bounces on his neck.*

BEHIND HIM *– we can hear a woman calling.*

MOTHER

Jimmy! Come back!

EXT. GRAVEYARD – DAY

The house backs on to a GRAVEYARD.

He runs through the gravestones – towards the CHURCH. *As he runs – he starts to* GLIMPSE INFECTED.

Through the gravestones. Through the yew trees.

INT. CHURCH – DAY

JIMMY *enters the church.*

Closes the heavy oak door behind him. Then – freezes.

At the far end of the church, he can hear a noise. A scuffling. Scratching. Gasping.

He steps forward, cautiously.

And sees – down the far length of the church, down the aisles –

– the VICAR.

JIMMY

. . . Dad?

The VICAR *is a large man. Bent over. Strange jerking movements, fitting through his body. Strangled noises, escaping from his throat.*

Then SUDDENLY, *the* VICAR'S *head* SNAPS AROUND.

Revealing his face. The mottled skin and bleeding nose and eyes of the INFECTED.

REVEAL –

– JIMMY *is gone.*

CUT TO –

INT. CHURCH/TOWER – DAY

– JIMMY *climbing a* LADDER.

To the bell tower. The spire.

INT. CHURCH/SPIRE – DAY

JIMMY *reaches the top of the ladder. There, he crawls beneath the* BELL –

– to one of the WINDOW SLITS, *at the top of the spire. Cautiously, he peers out.*

The GRAVEYARD *is now full of* INFECTED. THEN, *directly below* JIMMY –

– the INFECTED VICAR *bursts out of the church.* RUNNING.

Across the graveyard, to the HOUSE.

As the INFECTED VICAR *runs, the other* INFECTED *start to follow. The collective noun of infected:* A CONGREGATION.

As they reach the house, we see – JIMMY'S MOTHER *and* SISTER *leaving by the back door. Trying to flee.*

They don't get more than a few yards, before the INFECTED VICAR *and the* CONGREGATION *reach them.*

As the MOTHER *and* SISTER *start to scream –*

– JIMMY *closes his eyes. Clamping them shut.*

His hands close around the GOLD CRUCIFIX.

JIMMY
Father. Why have you forsaken me?

CUT TO BLACK.

TITLE:

28 YEARS LATER

CUT TO –

INT. SPIKE'S HOUSE/BEDROOM – DAWN

– a different ten-year-old boy. Also with his eyes closed. But he's peaceful. Asleep in bed.

This is SPIKE.

Soft dawn light pushes through the edges of the curtains.

On the bedside table, there is a SUPERHERO ACTION FIGURE. *It looks like it's had a lot of use.*

There is also a folding LOCK KNIFE, *and* DYNAMO FLASHLIGHT. *Beats pass on the sleeping boy. Then –*

– *SPIKE's dad, JAMIE, pads into the room.*

JAMIE is in his late thirties. He's a big guy. Looks like a farm worker. Beard and long hair.

JAMIE sits beside SPIKE.

SPIKE stirs, as JAMIE scrunches SPIKE's hair.

JAMIE

Good morning, lovely boy.

SPIKE

Morning, Dad.

JAMIE

Ready for today?

SPIKE

Yeah.

Beat. Then JAMIE nods.

JAMIE

Get dressed. I'll get breakfast ready.

INT. SPIKE'S HOUSE/BEDROOM – DAY

The curtains have been opened.

Outside the window, we can see the houses of a small English village. Over the rooftops of some of the houses, WIND TURBINES are slowly turning.

SPIKE kneels on the floor, and ties the laces on his boots with a double bow.

Then he pulls on a jacket. It's a little too big for him, and has been repaired more than once.

Then he takes a backpack, and puts a few things inside. A scarf, a pair of cycling gloves, and the flashlight.

He pauses over the SUPERHERO ACTION FIGURE. He wants to put it in.

Picks it up. Holds it. Puts it into the bag.

Then takes it out again, and places it back on the bedside table.

The last thing he does is slip the lock knife into his jeans pocket.

INT. SPIKE'S HOUSE/KITCHEN – DAY

JAMIE *is cooking on an Aga stove.*

In one pan, two eggs and two slices of bacon are frying. In another, potatoes and onions.

SPIKE *enters, carrying his backpack.*

JAMIE

Got flashlight, sweater, whistle, water bottle?

SPIKE

Yep.

JAMIE

Knife?

SPIKE *taps his pocket. Then takes a seat at the table.* JAMIE *starts spooning breakfast onto two plates.*

Only one of the plates gets bacon.

SPIKE*'s eyes light up when he sees the serving.*

SPIKE

We're having bacon? For breakfast?

JAMIE

Dave and Rosey brought it round last night.

SPIKE

. . . Why don't you have any?

JAMIE

I had some already. While I was cooking.

SPIKE

You're lying! Share!

SPIKE *picks up a piece of bacon and tosses it on to his dad's plate.*

JAMIE *picks it up and tosses it back.*

SPIKE *is about to re-throw it – but* JAMIE *lifts a hand.*

JAMIE

Spikey. It's all yours.

AT THAT MOMENT –

– there is a strange noise from upstairs.

It's a moaning sound. Which lifts up into a kind of cry. JAMIE *puts his fork down.*

I'll go see to Mum. You finish up.

JAMIE *exits.*

SPIKE *keeps eating, alone.*

INT. SPIKE'S HOUSE/STAIRS – DAY

SPIKE *climbs the stairs to the top landing.*

As he climbs, the cries from the MAIN BEDROOM *are continuing.*

He stops on the landing, at the door to his parents' bedroom. Through the door, he can see JAMIE *holding* ISLA, SPIKE'S *mother.*

ISLA *is kicking gently with her legs on the bed, as if trying to push away pain.*

JAMIE *is cradling her head and shoulders, and holding on to one of her hands.*

ISLA

I can't, Jamie, I can't –

JAMIE

You've got to ride it out.

ISLA

Jamie, no. I can't –

INT. SPIKE'S HOUSE/PARENTS' BEDROOM – DAY

SPIKE enters and sits on the bed, on the other side from JAMIE.

He holds on to his mum's other hand.

When ISLA feels SPIKE's small fingers intertwining with hers, she makes an effort.

She focuses through the pain. Turns to look at him. Her eyes glaze with the effort.

ISLA

Spikey.

SPIKE

Hi, Mum.

ISLA

My baby. I didn't mean to make a fuss. It's my head.

SPIKE

It's okay.

ISLA

It's just pounding.

SPIKE

I know.

SPIKE strokes her hand, and ISLA smiles. Calming.

Maybe it's the effect of seeing SPIKE, maybe because whatever causes her pain is naturally receding.

ISLA

Why don't you tell me how school was today?

SPIKE

I haven't been to school. It's the morning, Mum.

ISLA

Is it?

JAMIE releases ISLA.

JAMIE

Yeah, it's morning. And –

JAMIE pauses.

– Isla, if you remember. Spike's not going to school today.

ISLA

Why not? Is it the weekend already?

JAMIE

No. It's Monday.

ISLA looks distantly alarmed.

ISLA

. . . So why isn't he going to school?

JAMIE

We spoke about this. A few times.

ISLA

Spoke about *what*, Jamie?

JAMIE

Me and Spike are going out. Today is his first time.

ISLA

First time? Do you mean you're going off the island? To the mainland?

JAMIE

Yes.

ISLA tries to sit up in bed.

ISLA

What?

SPIKE

Mum, stay on the bed –

ISLA
(*to Jamie*)
What the fuck are you talking about? Have you gone fucking crazy?

JAMIE
Isla – don't swear –

ISLA
He's a fucking *baby.*

JAMIE
He's ten –

ISLA
Are you trying to kill our fucking baby? You cunt –

JAMIE
Spike –

SPIKE
It's okay –

ISLA
You crazy fucking sick baby-murderer –

JAMIE
(*to Spike*)
Can you go back downstairs, Spike –

SPIKE
No, Dad, you go down –

ISLA
If my dad were still here he'd skin you alive! BABY-MURDERER!

SPIKE
(*hard*)
Dad. Go.

JAMIE *gets up.*

ISLA *calls after him as he exits.*

ISLA

Cunt, cunt, cunt –

ISLA*'s eyes are mad. Semi-frenzied.*

SPIKE *leans forward. Puts himself in front of her gaze.*

SPIKE

Mum.

SPIKE *cuts through the frenzy.*

ISLA *abruptly stops. She stares at him. Confused. Then –*

ISLA

. . . Spikey?

SPIKE

Yes.

ISLA *wipes a hand at her face. She's flushed. Sweating.*

ISLA

What's going on? I'm hot. Why am I feeling so hot?

SPIKE

It's the weather.

ISLA

My head is . . .

She breaks off a moment. Glazes.

. . . pounding.

Beat.

SPIKE

Hey, Mum. Look.

SPIKE *reaches into his jacket pocket, and pulls out a wrap of folded kitchen cloth.*

Inside, there is the second strip of bacon.

I brought you some breakfast. I'll just leave it by the bed. Eat a bit when you feel like it.

SPIKE leans over and kisses his mum's cheek. Then he stands.

ISLA

Are you off?

SPIKE

Yeah.

ISLA

Where?

SPIKE

. . . School.

ISLA nods.

ISLA

Okay, Spikey. Love you.

SPIKE

I love you too, Mum.

INT. SPIKE'S HOUSE/KITCHEN – DAY

SPIKE enters the kitchen – to find his dad with another man. Older. Late sixties.

This is SAM.

He is holding a small RECURVE BOW in his hands. And on the table, there are two QUIVERS – one bigger, one smaller. Each filled with metal-tipped ARROWS.

SAM

Morning, kiddo. I just restrung this for you.

SPIKE

Did it need a restring?

SAM

Nope. Did it for my own sake, really.

JAMIE
(*quiet*)

He's going to be fine, Sam.

SAM *hands the bow to* SPIKE.

SAM

Have a draw, son. Feel the weight.

SPIKE *takes the bow.*

Holds his left arm out straight. Draws the string to his cheekbone. SAM *watches closely. So does* JAMIE. SPIKE *holds the bow rock solid.*

Three beats pass. Then SPIKE *eases then string back.*

No shake at all. Strong lad. That's another four pounds of pull than before.

AS THEY TALK –

– JAMIE *has put on his own backpack, and picked up his* RECURVE BOW.

He slips his QUIVER *onto his back, then gestures for* SPIKE *to do the same.*

SPIKE

Make sure Mum's okay, Sam.

SAM

I'll do everything I can for her. You just look after yourself.

SPIKE

I will.

EXT. SPIKE'S HOUSE – DAY

SPIKE *and* JAMIE *exit the house.*

As they walk away, there's a tapping on the upstairs window. SPIKE *looks up, and sees* ISLA. *Standing. Waving.*

SPIKE *waves back. And beams.*

ISLA *smiles back. Blows him a kiss.*

EXT. HOLY ISLAND/VILLAGE – DAY

JAMIE and SPIKE walk through the village on HOLY ISLAND.

Aside from the wind turbines, it essentially looks like any other English village – small stone houses, some in terraces.

But it doesn't feel quiet, or empty. It feels densely populated and full of life.

Clothes hang from lines across the streets. Most of the front doors are open, and people are gathered in small groups, talking, or eating breakfast.

As JAMIE and SPIKE walk, people call out or wave to them.

MAN

Go get 'em, Spike.

TEENAGE GIRL

(*chants*)

Spik-ey! Spik-ey!

A few people applaud them. A six-year-old girl runs up and gives SPIKE an apple.

GIRL

It's from Mum.

SPIKE looks over to the little GIRL'S house – where a husband and wife are standing. The HUSBAND is holding a young baby.

SPIKE

Thanks, Betty!

WIFE

Your big party tonight, our Spike! Don't you be late!

SPIKE waves.

SPIKE

I won't!

In one of the last buildings on the street, a pretty woman in her thirties approaches them from one of the buildings.

This is ROSEY.

DAVE, *her husband, watches from the door.*

As SAM *did,* ROSEY *embraces* SPIKE, *and kisses him.*

She smiles warmly at JAMIE *– and holds his gaze for one beat. Something private passes between the two of them.*

Interrupted as DAVE *calls.*

DAVE

Think you've got the weather on your side, boys.

JAMIE

Looks like.

JAMIE *taps* SPIKE'*s shoulder.*

Let's go.

EXT. HOLY ISLAND/FIELDS – DAY

JAMIE *and* SPIKE *have left the village area, and are walking along a road.*

On the left side is water. The sea.

And on the far side of the water, there is the MAINLAND.

On the right-hand side of the road are FIELDS. *Some sown with crops, some pasture where sheep and cattle graze.*

And beyond the fields, there is a rocky outcrop, on which a CASTLE *stands.* LINDISFARNE.

EXT. HOLY ISLAND/PERIMETER WALL – DAY

The road ends where the island starts to taper into a CAUSEWAY.

Blocking the causeway is a HIGH WALL, *built from wood and stone.*

In the shelter of the wall –

– there is a spreading ORCHARD *of fruit trees – apple and pear.*

A GATE *is set into the wall, wide enough to let a vehicle through.*

Either side of the gate are LOOKOUT TOWERS *– like small wooden church spires, each with a* BELL *hanging inside.*

And waiting at the bottom of the gate are four people.

One of them is JENNY *– a woman in her early seventies, and the leader of the Holy Island community.*

JAMIE *and* SPIKE *approach.*

JAMIE

Look at that, Spike. You got the whole leadership committee.

JENNY *smiles as* JAMIE *and* SPIKE *get near.*

JENNY

Had to see you off. We're all very excited for you.

JENNY *glances at* JAMIE.

Even though you know I feel he's a bit young. Thirteen or fourteen would be more in keeping with practice.

JAMIE

He's ready.

Beat.

Then JENNY *looks down at* SPIKE.

JENNY

You know the rules of our community, Spike. If you leave, you can come back. But if you don't come back, no one is permitted to go and find you. There are no rescues. There are no exceptions.

She crouches down, to look directly into SPIKE*'s eyes.*

It was something we learned the hard way, from all the people we lost in the past. So once you walk onto the mainland, you're on your own. Do you understand?

SPIKE

Yes, Jenny.

JENNY nods. Then rises.

She calls up to one of the people in the lookout shelters – ANTHONY.

JENNY

Seen anything this morning, Ant?

ANTHONY

Nothing. Fully quiet.

JENNY gestures.

JENNY

Then open up for them.

Two of the men with JENNY start pulling open the heavy gates – just enough to let JAMIE and SPIKE pass through.

ANTHONY

(*calls*)

Mind how you go, boys. Don't miss the tide.

Once through, the gate closes behind them.

EXT. CAUSEWAY – DAY

The CAUSEWAY. A single-lane road, with sea either side. The road is mostly broken to pieces, and strewn with seaweed and slick algae growth, stretching from Holy Island to the mainland.

JAMIE and SPIKE stand, facing the MAINLAND.

The GATE is a couple of hundred metres behind them.

JAMIE

So what's this, Spike?

SPIKE

The causeway.

JAMIE

Talk me through it.

SPIKE

It's the only way to the mainland. But it's only there in low tide. In high tide, the sea covers it.

JAMIE

Can we swim it in high tide?

SPIKE

No. Because the sea has a current, and it will pull us past the island, and then out to sea. And we'll drown.

JAMIE glances at SPIKE.

JAMIE

We've got about four hours until high tide. Are we doing this?

SPIKE looks up at his dad.

SPIKE

We can't go back now, Dad. Everyone will think I'm soft.

JAMIE

Yeah. They will. Come on, then.

They start walking.

EXT. SEA – DAY

From a distance, we watch the two figures cross the causeway.

EXT. HILLSIDE – DAY

A hillside, with long meadow grass, looking over long-abandoned fields, and spreading forest.

Everything in the landscape is green. Behind is the flat blue-black horizon of the sea.

In the long meadow grass, at the crest of the hill, JAMIE *and* SPIKE *appear.*

They stop. And take in the view.

SPIKE

It's so big.

SPIKE *looks at* JAMIE.

If we kept walking, would we get to a place where you can't see the sea?

JAMIE

Sure. You could walk for days or weeks without seeing the coast. But there's nothing out there, Spikey. Nowhere to aim for.

SPIKE

There's other villages.

JAMIE

None have anything we don't have.

Beat.

What else do you see out there?

Silence, as SPIKE *scans. Then he frowns.*

SPIKE

By the treeline.

JAMIE

Yep.

REVEAL –

EXT. TREELINE – DAY

– down by the treeline, from the undergrowth, a shape starts to emerge.

It is an INFECTED *variant.*

A male. And physically different from the infected we have been used to seeing in the past.

It has the same eye haemorrhage, and the leaking blood from nose and mouth. But instead of being adrenalinised, it is fat, fleshy and slow. It moves on all fours, with its head and stomach low to the ground. Almost sliding.

Its face is encrusted with dirt and earth. Aside from the haemorrhages, the eyes are also opaque with cataracts. It moves its head as if it is blind.

As it pulls itself into the meadow, it starts digging in the soil with long, broken fingernails.

It pulls fat earthworms out of the soil, and sucks them into a blistered, toothless mouth.

CUT TO –

EXT. HILLSIDE – DAY

– JAMIE *and* SPIKE.

JAMIE

A slug. One of the slow ones. Doesn't mean they aren't dangerous.

JAMIE *squints at the treeline.*

If there's one visible, there's probably a couple more in the trees.

JAMIE *glances at* SPIKE.

Your bow isn't strong enough for the chest. You need to hit it in the neck.

SPIKE *swallows.*

SPIKE

Yes, Dad.

JAMIE

You scared?

SPIKE

Only a little bit.

Beat.

. . . Are you?

JAMIE

No. We're good.

JAMIE *pulls an arrow from his quiver.*

Notch up. Let's get your first kill.

EXT. MEADOW – DAY

JAMIE *and* SPIKE *move slowly and quietly through the long grass, each with an* ARROW *notched in their bow.*

Around sixty feet from the SLUG, JAMIE *holds up a hand to stop.*

JAMIE
(*whispers*)

You like this range?

SPIKE *assesses. He looks nervous, but he's controlling himself.*

He nods.

JAMIE *scans the treeline again.*

(*whispers*)

He's yours. Anything that comes out after is mine.

SPIKE *nods.*

Then raises his small bow, and draws on the SLUG.

But he does not release. Instead, he lifts the bow. Steadily, certainly. Angling up.

Around SPIKE'S *legs, the wind blows the meadow grass gently to his left.*

He adjusts the bow slightly to the right.

JAMIE
(*continued*)

Send it.

SPIKE *releases.*

The ARROW *flies through the air. Dips. Curves slightly.*

Then PIERCES *the* SLUG'S *neck perfectly.*

The SLUG *rears up on its knees. Tries to stand.*

As it rises, we see that it is strangely coloured. Its underside flesh is milky white. Its topside is darkly tanned.

It staggers. Then makes a weird, strangled screaming noise. High-pitched, like a castrato.

MOMENTS LATER – *two more* SLUGS *appears from the* TREELINE. *A male and a female.*

These are standing. Lunging forward from the undergrowth. Making the same high scream.

ALMOST IMMEDIATELY – JAMIE *has fired an arrow at the* FIRST SLUG.

He hits it neatly in the chest.

The second SLUG *sees* JAMIE *and* SPIKE.

It puts on a burst of speed. Running across the meadow towards them.

JAMIE *is unfazed. He just notches another arrow.*

SPIKE watches, amazed by the sight, and his dad's fluidity and confidence.

JAMIE lets the SLUG make some of the distance between them. Not panicked. Not relaxed. Focused.

When ready, he releases. And again, the arrow hits the SLUG in the chest.

The high scream stops dead.

The SLUG stands upright a moment. Then topples, like a felled tree.

CUT TO –

– SPIKE. Breathing fast. Wide-eyed.

JAMIE
(*continued*)
Beautiful kill, Spike. You feel good?

SPIKE
. . . I think so.

JAMIE
You should. I'm proud of you.

JAMIE shoulders his bow.

Now we move. The screaming will have alerted other infected in the area.

EXT. FOREST – DAY

JAMIE and SPIKE make their way through forest, arrows notched.

INT. ABANDONED HOUSE – DAY

JAMIE and SPIKE enter the derelict remains of a house.

The interior is a rotten carcass. It also looks like it has been stripped of materials. Copper pipes are pulled out of the walls and floors.

JAMIE

Always worth looking around for something useful. People will have searched this place a hundred times, but – you never know.

SPIKE *picks up a couple of items of cutlery, from a half-collapsed kitchen cabinet.*

SPIKE

Are these useful?

JAMIE

No. We've got enough knives and forks. But . . .

JAMIE *reaches down, and picks something up from the floor. A plastic disc.*

. . . this is.

SPIKE

What is it?

JAMIE

A frisbee. I'll show you tomorrow when we get home. You'll love it.

He jams the frisbee into his backpack.

EXT. FIELDS – DAY

JAMIE *and* SPIKE *watch wild horses gallop across a meadow field.*

SPIKE

They're amazing . . .

JAMIE

Yeah.

The horses vault the remains of a drystone wall, and are gone.

CUT TO –

EXT. TREE – DAY

– a body, hanging upside down from a tree. Tied by a rope around its ankles.

REVEAL –

– JAMIE and SPIKE.

JAMIE is gazing up at the body. SPIKE isn't.

JAMIE

No. Don't look away, Spike. There's something for you to learn here.

Nervously, SPIKE looks up. And sees –

– the feet and legs are intact.

The lower torso has a letter, deeply carved into the stomach area.

Livid with black-red congealed blood, against milk-white skin: the letter J.

And the body's upper body is badly mauled.

The flesh on its head and hanging arms is ragged and torn. And the fingers on the hands are almost completely gone – as if they have been eaten off.

SPIKE swallows back his shock. Tries to sound collected.

JAMIE

(*continued*)

This is why our community is so precious.

Beat.

SPIKE

. . . What happened to him?

JAMIE

Looks like he got tied up. Then left for the infected.

SPIKE

But why would anyone do that?

JAMIE

A punishment? A warning? That letter J stands for something.

Beat.

But sometimes people just do evil just because they can. There's strange folk out here. Particularly the ones that roam.

SPIKE

. . . Is that the lesson?

JAMIE

The lesson is, however bad the infected are, people can be worse.

JAMIE *glances down at* SPIKE.

Okay. You've learned it. Let's keep going.

EXT. FOREST – DAY

JAMIE *and* SPIKE *move through the woods. Then –*

– JAMIE *stops. And* SPIKE *immediately does the same. Watches his dad for the next cue.*

JAMIE *touches a finger to his lips. Then gestures ahead.*

SPIKE *looks where* JAMIE *indicates. And sees – on the ferns ahead – specks of blood.*

EXT. FOREST CLEARING – DAY

A forest clearing.

In it, there are the bodies of two DEER. *They are more or less intact. They have been partially eaten, with hide pulled back and ragged flesh underneath.*

Their intestines and stomachs have been pulled from their bellies, and are strewn around the ground.

REVEAL JAMIE *and* SPIKE. *Looking at the carnage.*

JAMIE
(*quiet*)
This wasn't slugs, Spikey. This was the fast ones. Probably the same pack that did for that poor bastard we saw.

JAMIE *and* SPIKE *move closer to the bodies.*

(*quiet*)
Fresh. This morning. Make sure you don't touch the blood . . .

But SPIKE *has seen a third* DEER. *From his expression, there's something strange about it.*

SPIKE
(*whispers*)
Dad. What did they do to this one?

JAMIE *walks to where* SPIKE *stands.*

This DEER *is in a very different state. It is almost unrecognisable. The body has been torn to pieces, and the* HEAD *has been pulled away completely.*

And from the neck, a length of SPINE *is still attached.*

AS SOON AS HE SEES THE DEER HEAD AND SPINE – JAMIE'S *entire demeanour shifts.*

A sudden seriousness. In his eyes, we see fear.

He immediately lifts his bow. Scans the surrounding trees.

SPIKE
(continued; whispers)
What?

JAMIE
(whispers)
An Alpha did that.

INT. FOREST – DAY

JAMIE and SPIKE move through the woods. Quiet – but quicker than before.

JAMIE is ultra-alert. SPIKE is scared.

SPIKE
(quiet)
We're going back?

JAMIE
(quiet)
You got your kill.

SPIKE
(quiet)
Won't it look like we left early?

JAMIE
(quiet)
Don't talk, Spikey. Just keep your eyes peeled.

EXT. TREELINE – DAY

They reach the treeline, with the meadow and hillside beyond. Then, they stop.

JAMIE waits. Listening. Scanning.

Beats pass. But nothing changes, or moves.

JAMIE
(*quiet*)

Looks clear. Let's go.

They slip out from the treeline –

EXT. MEADOW – DAY

– into the meadow. Through the long grass, bows ready. Heading for the crest of the hillside that looks over the sea.

Then, halfway between the treeline and the crest – a shape appears on the top of the hill.

Silhouetted against the sky. An INFECTED MALE.

Its clothes have long rotted away. Its body is caked in years of unwashed dirt. The whites of its eyes are dark yellow, like tar-stained teeth, ringed with red. Blood has built up and crusted, like old lava flows, around its eyes and nose and corners of its mouth.

From its screaming mouth, we can see it has half of its teeth missing.

It has long matted hair and beard, and is freakishly etched with muscle – as if it has no fat on its body at all. All over its body, HERNIAS *and* VEINS *are unnaturally protruded, into dense ropes and knots.*

JAMIE *and* SPIKE *freeze at the sight.*

And a moment later – the INFECTED *is joined by* SIX OTHERS.

Male and female. In a line. Staring down the hillside at the father and son.

THEN *– a final figure appears. An* ALPHA. *It is massive. At least seven-foot tall.*

The infection has had a specific effect on the Alpha, as if the adrenalinised rage virus were a kind of intensely focused steroid/ growth hormone.

It looks like a nightmarish VIKING BERSERKER.

JAMIE

An Alpha. Fuck. Back to the trees, Spike! Go! *GO!*

JAMIE *and* SPIKE *start to run back to the treeline.*

The INFECTED *start to run in pursuit –* EXCEPT *the* ALPHA. *The* ALPHA *just stands. And watches.*

EXT. FOREST – DAY

JAMIE *and* SPIKE *run through the forest.*

Behind them, we can see the shapes of the INFECTED, *sprinting through the trees.*

But it's impossible for SPIKE *to run as fast as he needs to. He's too young. His legs are too short.*

JAMIE

DEFENCE!

They both STOP *and* TURN, *lifting their bows.* JAMIE *tracks the nearest* INFECTED. *Then shoots.*

The arrow flies between trees – and slams into the INFECTED'S *waist.*

As he re-notches the next arrow –

– SPIKE *is trying to aim at the next* INFECTED. *But it's fast, and he's panicking.*

He fires – and misses. The arrow lands harmlessly in the trunk of a tree.

A SPLIT SECOND LATER *– the same* INFECTED *is dropped by* JAMIE.

JAMIE
(*continued*)

MOVE!

They start running again.

Again, we glimpse the pursuing INFECTED *figures.*

DEFENCE!

They stop. Turn. And JAMIE *hits the next* INFECTED *in the leg. As* JAMIE *draws on it again –*

SPIKE *tries to aim his own bow – but is shaking uncontrollably. Breathing too fast.*

He releases his next arrow. This time, the arrow hits the INFECTED *in the upper arm.*

It does nothing – the INFECTED *doesn't react or break stride. A beat later,* JAMIE *hits the* INFECTED *that* SPIKE *has clipped.*

Then he re-notches on the INFECTED *he shot in the leg, which is still limping towards them.*

This time, JAMIE *hits it in the chest.*

MOVE!

JAMIE *has seen something ahead.* A TALL TREE. *He starts dragging* SPIKE *towards it.*

EXT. FOREST/TREE – DAY

At the base of the tree, JAMIE *grabs* SPIKE *and almost hurls him up to the first limb.*

JAMIE

CLIMB! CLIMB!

JAMIE *jumps up after* SPIKE, *and pulls himself up to the first limb – as the remaining two* INFECTED *reach the base of the tree.*

He shoots the first from directly above.

The arrow sinks straight down into the top of the shoulder, deep into the chest.

The last INFECTED *looks up – and* JAMIE *shoots an arrow directly into its mouth.*

It's his LAST ARROW.

EXT. FOREST/TREE/CANOPY – DAY

JAMIE *and* SPIKE *keep climbing until they reach near the top of the tree. Right up in the canopy.*

From here, perched where the branches split, they can see over the top of the carpet of forest.

A little distance away, they can see the MEADOW. *Beyond it, the* SEA. *Between the meadow and the sea, the* HILLSIDE.

And still standing there, on the crest of the hill, alone – the ALPHA.

JAMIE

It's waiting. Alphas aren't like the others. Not just bigger. Smarter.

SPIKE

What are we going to do?

JAMIE

We're not fighting it. I've got no arrows left, and anyway, I've seen it take a dozen hits to drop one of those things. So – we'll wait too.

Beat.

SPIKE

Is really no one going to come and help us? Even Sam?

JAMIE *shakes his head.*

JAMIE

Sam will want to come. But he won't. That rule can't be broken.

SPIKE

. . . I'm really sorry, Dad.

JAMIE

What about?

SPIKE

This is all my fault. And I couldn't hit anything. I tried but I was too scared and –

JAMIE

– Hey.

SPIKE meets his dad's gaze.

None of this is your fault. And you kept firing. I've seen adults who can't get an arrow in the bow, they're shaking so hard. You did well.

Silence, as they both watch the ALPHA – which remains motionless on the crest of the hill.

SPIKE

. . . We're going to miss the low tide, aren't we.

JAMIE

There'll be another.

EXT. CAUSEWAY – DAY

Water covers the causeway to HOLY ISLAND.

EXT. HILLSIDE – DUSK

The sun is dropping.

The ALPHA stands against the sky, in the orange light. Hulking. Almost motionless.

Then, abruptly – it turns. And walks away.

EXT. FOREST/TREE/CANOPY – NIGHT

Night. A nearly full moon lights the landscape.

JAMIE

Look out to sea.

JAMIE *points out to the dark expanse of water, where in the far distance, a light is blinking. Moving.*

Quarantine patrol. Probably French.

But SPIKE *is looking in the other direction. To the mainland. Where, far away, in the distance, there is an* ORANGE GLOW.

SPIKE

Dad . . . what's that?

JAMIE *looks. Sees the orange light. And reacts slightly.*

JAMIE

Fire.

SPIKE

Something's burning?

JAMIE

Something. Yeah.

JAMIE'S *tone indicates it's not something he wants to discuss. But* SPIKE *pushes.*

SPIKE

Is it another village?

JAMIE

No.

SPIKE

. . . What is it then?

JAMIE

I don't know. Never been there.

SPIKE

It always burns?

JAMIE

Often.

SPIKE

But –

JAMIE

– I just said I've never been there, Spike.

JAMIE's tone is final.

Silence. Then –

All right. Should be low tide by now. Time to move.

SPIKE

. . . Okay.

JAMIE

Once we get down, slow and quiet. If we see the Alpha, don't use the bow. You just run. Straight for the causeway and over it. You stop for nothing.

SPIKE

. . . Where will you be?

JAMIE

Behind you.

EXT. HILLSIDE – NIGHT

JAMIE and SPIKE creep up to the top of the hillside.

At the top, they can see down to the SEA, and HOLY ISLAND. Between the shoreline and HOLY ISLAND, there is only water.

JAMIE

No sign of the Alpha.

SPIKE

It's still high tide.

JAMIE

Only just. The water will be shallow. We can make it.

EXT. MAINLAND SHORE – NIGHT

Moonlit waves, black sand, and the old road to HOLY ISLAND, *running straight into the water.*

HOLY ISLAND *sits tantalisingly close. The lights of the village clearly visible.*

JAMIE *and* SPIKE *reach the point where the tarmac disappears into the water.*

JAMIE *steps forward – and sea comes up over his boots, but no more.*

JAMIE

Ankle-deep. We're good. All right, Spike. You go first.

They start walking out into the sea.

EXT. CAUSEWAY/HIGH TIDE – NIGHT

JAMIE *and* SPIKE *make their way across the causeway.*

JAMIE

How about that day, Spike. First time to the mainland. First kill. First run-in with infected. Saw an Alpha, and missed the tide!

SPIKE

We've got so much to tell Mum, when we get –

AT THAT MOMENT –

– from somewhere BEHIND THEM, *there is a low* ROAR. *Unnaturally deep.*

It sounds exactly like the guttural sound of LION.

SPIKE
(*continued*)

– home.

JAMIE knows exactly what the noise is.

He turns and sees – standing back on the beach, the ALPHA. There's half the distance of the causeway between them.

JAMIE

Run, Spike.

The ALPHA starts to SPRINT towards them.

RUN!

CUT TO –

– the PURSUIT across the causeway.

It's beautiful – in some ways. The moonlit night and water.

A dreamlike image – almost, but not quite, running across the surface of the water.

And nightmarish – the way the water slows them. Needing to run. Needing to be fast. Not being quite able.

INEVITABLY – the ALPHA is faster. Pounding through the shallow sea. Twice their speed.

And SPIKE is slow. The water harder for him. Slowing him more. Tripping him. Getting hauled up by JAMIE.

JAMIE
(*continued*)

Come on, Spike. Come on, come on.

As they start to near the WALL and GATE –

– JAMIE starts trying to shout.

OPEN UP! INCOMING! INCOMING!

SUDDENLY –

– BRIGHT ELECTRIC FLOODLIGHTS *turn on across the top of the* GATE, *illuminating the* CAUSEWAY.

And the WARNING BELLS *on the top of the* WATCHTOWERS *start* RINGING.

Now JAMIE *and* SPIKE *are running into blinding light. And the* ALPHA *is picked out perfectly.*

REVEALED *as being only seconds away from catching them.* JUST AS IT IS ABOUT TO GET A HAND TO THEM –

– JAMIE *launches himself at* SPIKE, *and* KNOCKS SPIKE FACE-DOWN *into the* WATER.

And a split second later – a VOLLEY *of* ARROWS *from the* GATE *start slamming into the* ALPHA.

In the space of two seconds – EIGHT ARROWS *have embedded themselves into the* ALPHA'S *torso and limbs.*

It stops dead in its tracks. Towering directly over JAMIE *and* SPIKE.

A beat later – another VOLLEY *shoots out of the blinding light. Turning the steroid-bulked creature into a pincushion.*

Then it topples backwards into the water with a heavy splash.

EXT. LINDISFARNE CASTLE/GROUNDS – NIGHT

A SHEEP *roasts on a spit, over open coals.*

REVEAL –

– a party in the grounds of the castle, in which SPIKE *is the guest of honour.*

The entire village has gathered around a STAGE, *in front of the castle.*

There are musicians on the stage – fiddle, guitar, drums – but they aren't playing. They are standing behind JAMIE *and* SPIKE.

JAMIE, clearly drunk, is addressing the entire crowd, with one hand holding a pint of CIDER, and the other resting on SPIKE's shoulder.

JAMIE

It's twenty-five, thirty yards. There's tall grass. A wind. And where does that arrow go? Right through its bloody neck.

JENNY applauds, and the CROWD give a huge cheer. In the crowd, we see ROSEY. Watching, beaming.

Fat bastard stands up, gives out one of those girly screams, then drops like a sack of fucking potatoes.

Another cheer. Even bigger.

CROWD

Get in there, our Spike!

SPIKE looks amazed, thrilled, and overwhelmed.

JAMIE

Next thing, we've got eight fucking infected –

SPIKE

Dad, swearing!

CROWD

Let him fucking swear, son!

JAMIE

– running right at us, fists pumping, eyes bulging. And he's turning, shooting. *Sending* it. Right to 'em.

SPIKE

No – I kept missing them!

JAMIE lifts SPIKE's hand.

JAMIE

Our Spike! Fucking giant killer!

The cheer is deafening.

CUT TO –

– the party in full swing.

Many of the adults are dancing. Among them, we find JAMIE.

SPIKE *is talking to kids in the village, who are gathered around him.*

A MAN *passes – and jams a glass of* CIDER *in* SPIKE'S *hand.*

SPIKE *tries to refuse, but the* MAN *won't take no. So* SPIKE *is forced to drink the glass, while the kids look on, laughing and applauding.*

We find JAMIE *again – who has started dancing with* ROSEY.

EXT. SEA – NIGHT

The moonlit sea near HOLY ISLAND.

The music from the party floats over the water.

In the foreground, the CORPSE *of the* ALPHA, *studded with* ARROWS, *drifts past, caught in the current.*

EXT. LINDISFARNE CASTLE – NIGHT

A little distance away from the party, SPIKE *heads for the bushes alone.*

The CIDER *has been a bit much for him. He gets to the bushes, and throws up.*

When he's finished, he wipes at his mouth. Breathes in the cool night air. Sobering up.

Takes a moment to himself. Looks up at the sky.

With no light pollution, the sky is a carpet of stars. The Milky Way is coloured.

A beat. Then SPIKE *starts walking back. Then – stops. Ahead, he's seen something.* JAMIE. *Also walking away from the party. With* ROSEY. *Hand in hand.*

They duck around the side of the castle wall. Unknowingly, in plain view of SPIKE.

They start to hurriedly kiss. SPIKE *is stunned.*

As JAMIE *pulls up* ROSEY'S *shirt, and* ROSEY *pulls at* JAMIE'S *trousers,* SPIKE *turns.*

And starts to run away.

INT. SPIKE'S HOUSE/KITCHEN – NIGHT

SPIKE *enters the kitchen, to find* SAM, *sat at the table. Reading.*

SAM *puts the book down. Looks surprised.*

SAM

Spike? Back from your party? Didn't think I'd see you until past midnight.

SPIKE

I wanted to see Mum.

SAM

She's sleeping, son.

SPIKE

. . . Was she okay today?

SAM

Better than okay. She was up and about. We walked to the fields. She's got a lot of life in her, when she isn't having a turn.

SAM *smiles.*

But what about *your* day, more to the point. Tell me about it. I was scared to death when I heard you missed the tide.

SPIKE *sits opposite* SAM.

SPIKE

I don't know. Dad's making it out to be something it's not.

SAM

Like what?

SPIKE

Like I'm a hero.

SAM

I'm sure you are, to him.

SPIKE

(*quiet*)

Feels like he's lying.

Beat.

SAM

So what did happen today?

SPIKE *shrugs.*

SPIKE

I shot one of the fat ones. It was hardly moving. Then we got attacked by fast ones, and I couldn't hit a thing. Then we climbed a tree, and hid until it got dark.

Beat.

I was just scared. Felt sick. Just wanted to be home with Mum.

SAM

Your dad probably felt the same.

SPIKE *lets that go. Changes the subject.*

SPIKE

I'd never seen so much land, Sam. Couldn't believe it was so big.

SAM

. . . What did you see?

SPIKE

Land. Hills. Forest.

Beat.

And a fire.

SAM

A fire?

SPIKE

When it got dark.

SAM

Huh. I wonder if you saw old Kelson. Didn't imagine he was still alive. Was it south-west?

SPIKE *nods.*

Yep. That's probably Kelson. Believe it or not, he was my GP, some thirty years back.

SPIKE

. . . What's a GP?

SAM

A doctor.

A doctor. A beat. On SPIKE.

SPIKE

A doctor?

SAM

Yup. Had his practice just outside Whitley Bay.

SPIKE *watches* SAM.

SPIKE

Dad said he didn't know what the fire was. And he says all real doctors are dead. That's why no one knows what's wrong with Mum.

SAM *looks uncomfortable.*

Feels like he's lying about everything.

SAM

You know what? Maybe he didn't want to spook you. Doctor Kelson is . . . odd.

SPIKE

How is he odd? What's so special about the fire?

SAM

I'm sorry, son. If your dad doesn't want to talk about it, I don't think I should.

Beat.

Why don't you go back to the party? I'm fine here with your mum. And she's fine with me.

SPIKE

No, you go. I'll look after her now.

SPIKE *looks at* SAM.

I want to, Sam. I've missed her.

Beat. Then SAM *nods.*

SAM

(gentle)

Okay.

INT. SPIKE'S HOUSE/PARENTS' BEDROOM – NIGHT

SPIKE *creeps into his parents' bedroom.*

ISLA *is on the bed. As* SAM *described her: peaceful, asleep. The bacon still sits on the side table.*

SPIKE *slips his shoes off, and crawls into bed next to her.*

She stirs, and drops her arm around him. And SPIKE *closes his eyes.*

INT. SPIKE'S HOUSE/PARENTS' BEDROOM – DAWN

SPIKE *wakes – to hear* ISLA *softly moaning beside him.*

SPIKE

Mum?

SPIKE holds ISLA's hand.

ISLA

Spike. Go to the shops, will you? I need some Nurofen.

SPIKE

Nurofen?

ISLA

For my head. Just –

ISLA breaks off. Maybe half-remembering – there are no shops. No Nurofen.

Never mind. It doesn't matter.

ISLA rises. Swings her legs out of bed. She's weak, but not unsteady on her feet.

SPIKE

Where are you going?

ISLA

Bathroom.

ISLA exits.

A few moments later, SPIKE hears the sound of ISLA peeing. Then – suddenly – retching.

Then a few beats after that, the sound of a water pail being poured into the toilet bowl.

ISLA returns. She climbs back into bed, and puts an arm around SPIKE.

ISLA
(*continued*)

So what's your plan today?

Beat.

SPIKE

. . . No plan, really.

ISLA

No school?

SPIKE

No.

ISLA *smiles faintly.*

ISLA

Whenever I had a day off school, your grandpa would take a day off work. He'd put a sign on his fishing boat that said 'Gone Fishing'. And then we'd go into town.

AT THAT MOMENT – *from* DOWNSTAIRS, *there is the sound of the front-door latch turning. Then the door closing.*

Is that Dad getting back from work?

JAMIE
(*offstage; calls*)

Hullo!

ISLA

. . . We're up here, love.

Footsteps on the stairs.

Then JAMIE *appears at the bedroom door. He looks a little worse for wear.*

JAMIE

Well. That was some party.

ISLA

You look –

ISLA *breaks off. Something is on the tip of her tongue – but it takes her a moment to find it.*

– as if you got dragged through a hedge backwards.

JAMIE

Maybe I did. I woke in the wheat field.

JAMIE looks at SPIKE.

Where did you disappear to, Spikey? Looked around and the guest of honour had vanished.

SPIKE

(*flat*)

Just came home.

JAMIE picks up on the vibe from SPIKE – but maybe is too hungover to make much sense of it.

JAMIE

I'll make us some breakfast.

INT. SPIKE'S HOUSE/KITCHEN – DAY

JAMIE pushes scrambled eggs around in a pan, on the wood stove.

SPIKE enters. Sits at the table. And watches his dad. JAMIE turns.

JAMIE

What's going on, Spike?

SPIKE

Why didn't you tell me there was a doctor that could see Mum?

JAMIE

Doctor? We don't have a doctor. Haven't had a doctor here in forever.

SPIKE

Doctor Kelson. The fire. On the mainland.

JAMIE frowns.

JAMIE

Who've you been talking to?

SPIKE

So he is a doctor.

JAMIE

Was it Sam? Bloody fool. Putting ideas in your head.

SPIKE waits.

He's not a doctor, Spike. Maybe he once was. Years ago. But he's long since gone insane.

SPIKE

What do you mean?

JAMIE shakes his head.

Is he a doctor or not?

JAMIE sighs.

JAMIE

Before you were born, we used to forage. But it got harder, so you'd have to travel further. And one day, it took a group of us close to Kelson's.

Beat.

Five hundred yards out, we started to smell death. And understand, we were well-used to that smell. Back then, the dead were everywhere. But this was totally different. This stench was like a wall. Like you could touch it.

Beat.

We got to the brow of this hill, looked down, and – I'd never seen anything like it.

JAMIE glazes at the memory.

Corpses. Hundreds. Arranged in lines. Men, women, children. And right in the middle, there was a fire. And stood by it, was Kelson. For some unfathomable purpose, he'd dragged all the bodies there.

Beat.

A few seconds later, Kelson turned and looked right at us. Then – he waved. Casually. Like – hi, guys. Come down.

Beat.

We turned and ran. And in fifteen years, none of us have ever been back.

JAMIE exhales.

Like I said. Insane.

Silence. Then –

Fuck.

JAMIE spins around, to find the eggs are burned. Black. JAMIE pulls them off the heat. Gazes at them.

He suddenly looks defeated. Vacant.

A beat, as SPIKE watches the back of his dad's head.

SPIKE

Do you want Mum to die?

JAMIE

Course I don't. What a question.

SPIKE

What's really wrong with her?

JAMIE

I don't know.

SPIKE

Is she dying?

JAMIE

I don't *know*, Spike.

SPIKE

I think she is dying. So do you.

JAMIE says nothing. Just keeps gazing at the blackened pan.

If she dies, are you going to be with Rosey?

JAMIE *freezes. Then turns.*

JAMIE

Spike. Watch your mouth.

SPIKE

What would her Dave say about that?

JAMIE *steps forward – and lashes out with the flat of his hand. Clips* SPIKE *hard around the side of the face.*

JAMIE

I said – *watch your bloody mouth.*

JAMIE *stares at* SPIKE. SPIKE*'s eyes are brimming.* AT THAT MOMENT – ISLA *cries out from upstairs.*

SPIKE *stands.*

Son –

SPIKE *exits. Leaving* JAMIE *alone.*

INT. SPIKE'S HOUSE/PARENTS' BEDROOM – DAY

SPIKE *tries to soothe* ISLA. *She's writhing on the bed sheets.*

ISLA

It's pounding, Spike. Pounding.

SPIKE

I know, Mum. I'm sorry. I'm really sorry.

JAMIE *appears at the door. Watches. He looks helpless.*

JAMIE

Do you need water, love? I'll get you some.

SPIKE *gets off the bed, and moves towards his dad, and pushes* JAMIE *back, out of the doorway –*

INT. SPIKE'S HOUSE/LANDING – DAY

– to the top landing.

SPIKE

Get the fuck away from us.

JAMIE

From 'us'?

SPIKE reaches into his back pocket, and flips out the blade of his pocket knife. Holds it out at his dad.

SPIKE

You heard me.

JAMIE's hand flashes out. Grab's SPIKE's wrist. Prises the knife out.

Then folds the blade, and hands it back to him. SPIKE takes it. Humiliated, but unbowed.

Go away, Dad.

A beat.

Then JAMIE turns, and goes.

SPIKE watches his dad walk down the stairs, then leave through the front door.

HOLD *on* SPIKE'S FACE.

Behind him, ISLA is crying out again. But SPIKE doesn't move. Just stares.

CUT TO –

EXT. HOLY ISLAND/BARN – DAY

– FIRE. Blazing.

It's a barn, on the edge of a field, between the village and Lindisfarne Castle. Fully alight, with dark smoke and jets of orange flame billowing into the air.

FROM *the village – people are* RUNNING *towards the blaze. We can hear their shouts.*

CROWD

Fire!

CUT TO –

EXT. HOLY ISLAND/PERIMETER WALL – DAY

– ANTHONY, *in the lookout tower, staring at the rising plume of smoke across the fields.*

ANTHONY

Fucking smoke. Look.

AT THAT MOMENT – below, SPIKE *comes running up.*

SPIKE

Ant! Jess! Fire in the main barn! They said they need everybody! You've got to go and help!

ANTHONY

We can't leave the gate, Spike!

SPIKE

That's why they sent me! I'll be on the bell! They need every man, they said!

ANTHONY *and* JESS *exchange a glance.*

CUT TO –

– ANTHONY *and* JESS, *running away from the* GATE, *across the fields.*

SPIKE *watches them. Then –*

EXT. HOLY ISLAND/PERIMETER WALL/ORCHARD – DAY

– walks to the apple and pear ORCHARD, *that lies in the shelter of the* PERIMETER WALL.

Where ISLA *is sitting beneath one of the trees.*

SPIKE

Come on, Mum. Let's go.

EXT. CAUSEWAY – DAY

SPIKE *and* ISLA *walk across the causeway, to the* MAINLAND.

EXT. ROAD – DAY

SPIKE *and* ISLA *walk along a single-lane road.*

The unchecked foliage has grown so much on either side that there is only a narrow band of broken-up tarmac remaining.

SPIKE *is scanning and listening as they move. He has his bow out, and an arrow notched.*

ISLA *looks physically tired, and distracted. Talking quietly to herself. Illegible.*

Then the foliage either side of the road opens out.

They are passing the remains of an old country PUB.

Fully derelict. Overrun with ivy. No glass left in the windows. But the sign is still visible.

ISLA

No one at the pub today. No one enjoying a pint in the sunshine.

ISLA *stops, arrested by the sight.*

Look, Spikey. If you screw up your eyes, you can almost see what it was like –

ISLA *cuts off. Frowns.*

Before . . .

ISLA *turns to her son.*

. . . This is the mainland.

SPIKE

. . . Yes.

ISLA

But – we can't be on the mainland. It's too dangerous. It's –

SPIKE

– It's okay, Mum. I know how to keep us safe.

ISLA *starts to panic.*

ISLA

No. No, *no*! This isn't right. It's *not* right.

(*breaks off*)

Where's Jamie? Where's Dad?

SPIKE

Dad's not here.

ISLA

Then we have to get back now. Back home. We have to – run, or –

SPIKE

We can't get back, Mum. Not now. The tide will have come up.

ISLA'S *voice is rising. And a trickle of blood has started to run out of* ISLA'S *nose.*

ISLA

Oh God – oh God – but – why are we here? Why are we on the mainland?

SPIKE

Mum.

SPIKE *grabs her hand.*

We're going to the doctor.

ISLA

. . . Doctor?

SPIKE

A real doctor. From the old days.

SPIKE reaches up, and wipes ISLA's nose blood with his sleeve.

ISLA

. . . There's something wrong with me, isn't there, Spike.

SPIKE

Yes. I think there is, Mum. But the doctor's going to make you better.

ISLA stares at her son.

ISLA

. . . Okay.

CUT TO –

EXT. VALLEY – DAY

– the FACE of an EMACIATED INFECTED.

REVEAL –

– the INFECTED is agonisingly thin. At the edge of collapse and death from starvation.

Starvation has pulled its lips over its teeth in a skull grin. Its bloodied eyes seem bulging and outsized. Its skin is stretched over its bones.

It walks forward with halting, tottering steps.

As it moves forward, we REVEAL the view at the bottom of a valley.

A RUINED ABBEY. *Not ruined twenty-eight years ago. Ruined five hundred years ago.*

CUT TO –

EXT. RIVERBANK – DAY

– *the* FACE *of an* INFECTED WOMAN.

She is standing knee-deep in water. And she is over eight months PREGNANT.

Around her is a large group of INFECTED, *either standing in the water, or on the riverbank. Some appear to have large, unexplained tumours. Some carry injuries – strange limps, or are dragging broken limbs.*

Most are drinking from the river, like an animal herd.

The PREGNANT INFECTED *stands still, among the other thrashing forms.*

CUT TO –

EXT. ROAD – DAY

– *the* FACE *of an* ALPHA.

This ALPHA, *we will learn later, is called* SAMSON. *But for now, he is advancing towards us, and towards* GUNSHOTS.

REVEAL –

– *the* ALPHA *is moving on an old A-road, through the remains of cars. Once a gridlock of vehicles. Now barely recognisable. Rusted and skeletal.*

Also on the road are the bodies of several INFECTED *– who have been shot.*

And two other men, in military uniform.

REVEAL –

– ahead, a small group of SWEDISH MILITARY, *who are scattered amongst the rusted vehicles, defending themselves against an* INFECTED *attack.*

Two of the soldiers – ANDERS (23) *and* ERIK (22) *are firing. The last soldier,* NILS (26), *has run out of ammunition.*

As he tries to reload, the ALPHA *reaches him. It reaches down, and grabs* NILS' *head. Then lifts him into the air.*

More INFECTED *rush past the* ALPHA, *to* ANDERS *and* ERIK *–*

– as the ALPHA *holds* NILS' *shoulder with one hand, and pulls* NILS' *head with the other – and literally pulls* NILS' *head from his body.*

NILS' *spine, still attached to the head, seems to* UNZIP *from the back of his torso.*

The ALPHA *drops the limp body. Then moves at* ANDERS, *and attacks.*

He smashes down at ANDERS, *using* NILS' *head as a club. The bloody spine flails through the air like a whip.*

ERIK *turns and starts to run, as the berserker* ALPHA *howls.*

CUT TO –

EXT. FIELDS – LATE AFTERNOON

– SPIKE *and* ISLA, *walking through long grass and meadow flowers.*

The sun is getting low in the sky, and ISLA *is dragging her feet. Looking a little dazed.*

ISLA

Spike. Every step hurts my head.

SPIKE *looks round at her. Sees how badly she's struggling.*

SPIKE

Okay, Mum. Maybe we should stop for the night.

They have reached the top of a valley.

REVEAL –

– at the bottom of the valley, the RUINED ABBEY.

We'll stay there.

EXT. RUINED ABBEY – SUNSET

Only the walls and arches of the abbey still stand. SPIKE *and* ISLA *sit in what was once the main hall.*

ISLA *drinks from a water bottle, as* SPIKE *cuts an apple into slices with his penknife.*

ISLA

Spike. Is Dad silly?

SPIKE

. . . Dad?

ISLA

Yes. Silly with you. Jokey.

ISLA *lies down. Through the missing roof of the abbey, the clouds are catching the sunset.*

Your grandpa was *very* silly. You wouldn't believe how much. Everyone else thought he was so serious, but around me, he was daft.

Beat.

Is Dad like that, when it's just the two of you?

SPIKE

. . . No.

ISLA

Well. He's just wanting to make sure you're tough enough. Like him.

Beat.

When I look in your face, I can see your grandpa's eyes. It's nice.

SPIKE *looks at her. And crosses his eyes.*

ISLA *laughs.*

Exactly.

Beat.

SPIKE

Why don't you sleep? I'm going to stay awake. Keep watch.

ISLA

Okay, Dad.

SPIKE *looks at his mum, to see if she's joking, or confused. But she's already closed her eyes.*

SPIKE *takes off his jacket, and places it over her.*

EXT. RUINED ABBEY – NIGHT

Night has fallen. ISLA *sleeps, beneath* SPIKE*'s jacket.*

A little distance away, SPIKE *stays awake, sitting on the stone slab of the central* ALTAR. *Keeping guard. Holding his bow and arrow. But – he's exhausted.*

His chin keeps dropping. Eyelids sinking. SPIKE *jolts awake.*

But the next time his chin goes down – he doesn't jolt awake. He sinks down onto the altar, and falls asleep.

CUT TO –

– SPIKE *and* ISLA, *both asleep.*

SPIKE, *one hand still clutched around his bow, looks oddly reminiscent of the sleeping knights on medieval tombs.*

A beat passes.

Then – the EMACIATED INFECTED *appears. Stepping through the arches.*

In the moonlight, it looks like a hellish apparition. The imprint of a human, or a ghost.

It takes another step – not apparently having seen SPIKE *or* ISLA.

SPIKE *stirs in his sleep.*

The INFECTED *reacts. Its head flicks round to the altar – woken from its starvation stupor. A last trace of adrenalin activating in its system.*

Its fingers flex into claw shapes. Then it starts to advance on the sleeping boy.

Halting steps grow faster. More certain. Then – just as it is about to reach SPIKE –

– SPIKE'S JACKET *wraps around its head.*

Held by ISLA. *The material of the jacket bunched in each of her fists.*

ISLA *drags the* EMACIATED INFECTED *backwards.*

Swings it round. Then propels its head into one of the pillars that support the arches.

Its head is smashed against the stone corner. Then pulled back. And smashed again.

Each impact makes a sickening thump.

Over on the ALTAR – SPIKE *continues to sleep soundly.*

CUT TO –

– ISLA's face. We can see the same madness that we see in the faces of the INFECTED. Teeth bared and gritted. Eyes wide, as if in horror at herself.

Blood starts to seep through the material of the jacket.

ISLA smashes the INFECTED one more time. Then releases one hand from the material of the jacket.

The dead INFECTED slides down, and crumples to the floor. Its face is caved in.

ISLA lets the blood-soaked jacket drop. Then – walks to SPIKE. And climbs onto the ALTAR, lies beside him, and drapes an arm over his chest.

EXT. VALLEY/RUINED ABBEY – PRE-DAWN

The sun has not yet risen, but the sky is becoming light, filling the landscape with a strange cool glow that is neither bright nor dark, neither night nor day.

SPIKE wakes in ISLA's arms.

He sits up. Rubs at his eyes. Orientating himself.

Then he sees the body of the EMACIATED INFECTED, lying only a few metres away.

SPIKE grabs his bow.

SPIKE
(*whispers*)
Mum. What happened?

ISLA stirs. Opens her eyes.

ISLA
. . . Where?

SPIKE points at the corpse, folded by the archway pillar.

ISLA *stares at it blankly. Then back at Spike. Equally blankly.*

I don't know.

EXT. VALLEY – DAWN

Dawn breaking, at the top of the valley.

The two small figures of SPIKE *and* ISLA *make their way up the slope.*

In the distance, but closer than before, we can see smoke from DR KELSON'S FIRE, *rising.*

EXT. FIELDS – DAY

SPIKE *and* ISLA *walk through long grass. Waist-height.* ISLA *seems a little dazed, but not in pain.*

The landscape around them is entirely green, except for ONE *structure. Half a mile away, there is a* CHURCH SPIRE. *It rises over the treetops. The only human-made artefact in the landscape.*

The sight of it makes ISLA *stop.*

ISLA

Oh look. A church.

ISLA *smiles.*

Do you know what this reminds me of? That time we were walking in the countryside, and you pointed at a church spire, over treetops.

SPIKE *looks round, puzzled.*

It was *just* like this. Where we stood, we couldn't see any other buildings. No village, or road. Just the spire. And you turned to me, and said – if we were walking here five hundred years ago, this is exactly what we'd have seen. That spire, over trees. The same view. Unchanged.

SPIKE *stops walking, looking at* ISLA.

ISLA *stops too. She's looking past* SPIKE, *as if he isn't there.*

Do you remember that day? I couldn't have been more than seven or eight. Us two are real-life time-travellers, you said. We've fallen into the past. And I got scared, because I thought you were being serious. And we really had.

ISLA *gazes out at the green landscape – and, as happened before, a trickle of blood spills out of* ISLA*'s nose.*

How many hundreds of years have we fallen this time? Is it thousands? Or more.

SPIKE

. . . Mum?

ISLA *looks at* SPIKE. *She is confused for a moment, at the sight of him.*

ISLA

. . . Spike?

Then she smiles.

Spike.

SPIKE

. . . Your nose is bleeding again.

He steps over to her, and wipes away the blood.

Why does that keep –

SPIKE *cuts off.*

He has just seen something. BEHIND ISLA *– the long meadow grass is rippling. Similar to the way water is disturbed as something swims beneath the surface.*

SPIKE *watches the movement. Then looks back at* ISLA, *and lifts a finger to his own lips.*

SPIKE *takes a careful step forward. Then another.*

Then SEES *– the fleshy, mottled back of a* SLUG INFECTED. *Only three metres in front of him.*

He freezes. Lifts his bow. Notches an arrow.

THEN SEES –

another section of shifting grasses. A few metres further ahead.

SPIKE*'s gaze flicks to the left. There is another. He looks right. And sees another.*

REVEAL –

– a large group of SLUGS *are approaching them. A dozen of them, moving slowly through the meadow.*

SPIKE *and* ISLA *have strayed, without realising, into a kind of* HERD.

CUT TO –

– one of the SLUGS. *Its cataract-hazed eyes stare blindly ahead as it slowly claws through the meadow.*

CUT TO –

– SPIKE, *turns to* ISLA.

CUT TO –

SPIKE
(*mouths*)

Don't move.

– the cattle-like herd of SLUGS, *growing closer. Creeping forward. Wheezing as they breathe, sucking over toothless mouths as they eat up earthworms and beetles.*

The trajectory of TWO *of the* SLUGS *means they are about to pass either side of* SPIKE *and* ISLA.

CUT TO –

– SPIKE. *He takes his mother's hand.*

Then takes a deep breath. And looks in her eyes, keeping her calm, as the SLUGS *reach them.*

Mounds of suppurating flesh. Passing either side of their legs.

THEN – *one of the* SLUGS, *trailing its fingers along the surface of the ground –*

– finds the shoelace of ISLA*'s boot.*

It STOPS. *Pulls at the shoelace. And – the shoelace unties.*

Thinking it might have found food, the SLUG *moves its mouth down, and sucks the shoelace into its mouth.*

Then – REACTS. *As the shoelace grows taut. Its hand reaches again – and finds* ISLA*'s shoe.*

Immediately, the SLUG *tenses up. The touch turns into a* GRAB.

It lifts its head, and opens its mouth – about to make the high SLUG *scream.*

But is CUT DEAD *by an arrow in the throat, fired at point-blank range, from* SPIKE'S BOW.

The scream turns into a gurgle, as the SLUG*'s mouth fills with blood.*

But the noise is enough for all the other SLUGS *to react.*

They rise up, blind, but listening. Their heads all turning in the direction of the sound.

SPIKE *grabs* ISLA*'s arm.*

SPIKE
(*continued*)

Run!

SPIKE *and* ISLA *start* SPRINTING.

As they do so – the SLUGS *start screaming.*

AS THE SLUGS START SCREAMING – FIVE INFECTED *burst out from the* TREELINE *at the edge of the meadow.*

EXT. FIELDS – DAY

SPIKE *and* ISLA *run through the meadow –*

– as the INFECTED *start to run in pursuit.*

The INFECTED *are not in a tight group. One is some distance ahead of the other four.*

It isn't going to be possible for SPIKE *and* ISLA *to outrun them.*

EXT. PETROL STATION – DAY

Off the fields, the ruins of a petrol station and HAPPY EATER *café sit, with an overgrown road beyond it.*

SPIKE *and* ISLA *run onto the forecourt.*

The LEAD INFECTED *is only forty feet behind him.* SPIKE *stops. Turns. Lifts his bow.*

He aims at the LEAD INFECTED.

Unlike the attack in the forest, he doesn't panic. He focuses. He lets the INFECTED *get closer. Tracking the* INFECTED *the entire time.*

Thirty feet of distance between them. Twenty-five. Twenty.

At FIFTEEN FEET, SPIKE *releases – and the arrow shoots straight into the* LEAD INFECTED'S *neck.*

Momentum keeps the LEAD INFECTED *going, as blood fountains out around the arrow.*

Then it crashes to the forecourt, REVEALING *the other four* INFECTED, *following behind.*

SPIKE

In here! Go, Mum, go!

SPIKE *starts pulling* ISLA *towards the* HAPPY EATER *restaurant.*

INT. PETROL STATION/HAPPY EATER – DAY

SPIKE *pulls* ISLA *into the restaurant.*

The interior is rotten, and wrecked. The roof has half collapsed.

SPIKE *desperately tries to push the door closed – but the hinges are rusted, and it remains ajar.*

SPIKE

Mum – hide somewhere –

ISLA *doesn't move.*

ISLA

I'm scared.

She sounds like a child.

SPIKE *tries to block the door shut with an upended table.*

SPIKE

Mum, please – hide –

ISLA

No – no –

But the table is small, and light. And almost as soon as he has got it in place – the door is KICKED OPEN *by the* INFECTED.

No – no – no –

The other three INFECTED *are right behind.*

As he backs away, SPIKE *lifts his bow and notches an arrow.*

He fires as the INFECTED *charges. And again – hits the* INFECTED *in the neck.*

But the three behind burst through the door. SPIKE *drops his bow and backs away –*

– pulling out his LOCK KNIFE. *Putting himself between the three* INFECTED *and* ISLA.

A frozen beat. The three INFECTED. *The young boy, holding his small lock knife in front of him. His mother behind, arms bunched by her sides, curling into herself.*

Then the INFECTED *charge.*

And a beat later – a GUNSHOT *rings out.*

The first INFECTED *drops. Shot in the head.*

ABOVE THEM – *silhouetted against the sky, by the collapsed roof, the Swedish soldier,* ERIK, *is standing.*

Firing down with an ASSAULT RIFLE.

Two more shots. Deafening in the enclosed space. The last two INFECTED *are hit, and drop.*

SPIKE *looks up, amazed, confused.*

ERIK *looks down. Then dips the barrel of his gun.*

SPIKE

. . . Hello.

ERIK *continues gazing at them.*

. . . I'm Spike. This is my mum.

Beat.

ERIK

I'm Erik.

CUT TO –

EXT. ROAD – DAY

– the bodies of the Swedish soldiers – NILS *and* ANDERS. *Five* INFECTED *are crouched over the bodies, eating them. One of them is the* PREGNANT WOMAN.

As she eats – she suddenly breaks off. And tenses. We realise – she's having a contraction.

She rises. Stands. And starts to walk away from the bodies.

As she passes one of the rusting car carcasses, another contraction hits her.

AS SHE CRIES OUT, CUT TO –

INT. PETROL STATION/HAPPY EATER – DAY

– ISLA, *crying out. She is curled on the floor of the* HAPPY EATER, *lost in the pain of her headache, with* SPIKE *kneeling beside her, holding her hand.*

ERIK *stands over them. He looks wired.*

ERIK

What's wrong with her?

SPIKE

I don't know. I'm taking her to a doctor.

ERIK *goes to the door. Shoulders his rifle. Peers out.*

ERIK

What happens now?

SPIKE

What do you mean?

ERIK

You live here, don't you? On this fucking island. You're a native.

SPIKE

. . . A native?

ERIK

(*snaps*)

What happens now? Do more infected come?

SPIKE *looks at* ERIK. *Confused.*

SPIKE

. . . I don't know. Probably. They'll have heard the noise.

ERIK

Of course. More will come. The *bärsärk* will come. And rip our fucking heads off.

ON SPIKE – *the penny has dropped.*

SPIKE

You aren't from here.

ISLA *cries out again.*

ERIK

Jesus Christ. Please shut her up.

SPIKE

Where are you from?

ERIK

Sweden. Now shut her up.

SPIKE

She can't help it.

ERIK

She can't help it. You can't help me. Why did I help you? A fucking child and a dying woman.

SPIKE

She's *not* dying.

ERIK

I could have saved my bullets. Fuck. I should leave right now.

SPIKE

You can go. I'm not leaving my mum.

But ERIK *doesn't move from the door.*

ISLA

(*murmurs*)

My head. My head.

SPIKE *holds her hand tighter.*

SPIKE

I know.

ISLA

(*murmurs*)

Thank you, Daddy.

ERIK *looks back at them. Incredulous.*

ERIK

Could this get any more fucked up?

EXT. COUNTRYSIDE – DAY

SPIKE, ISLA *and* ERIK *make their way across the landscape.*

ERIK *is carrying* ISLA *on his back. He's not finding it easy. But his manic energy is helping.*

ERIK

My best friend from school is a delivery driver. You don't even know what a delivery driver is. He delivers packages. People buy things online, and –

(*breaks off*)

– you don't know what online is. It doesn't matter. He's a driver. And I told him – you're wasting your life, Felix. You get one life, and you're pissing it away. And he said, what are you going to do, fuck-nuts? So I joined the navy to prove a point. Now who's pissed away their life?

SPIKE

. . . I don't understand what you're saying.

ERIK

I'm saying I should have been a delivery driver. Right now, I'd be stuck in traffic, or driving too fast down a narrow street.

SPIKE

But why are you *here*?

ERIK

My fucking boat sank. We were patrolling the east coast of Scotland and hit something. Scotch on the rocks. Some of us got to a life raft. We didn't want to go to shore, *obviously*. But the wind blew us. Eight of us got to land. Now I'm the only one left.

SPIKE

. . . Will you be rescued?

ERIK *laughs bleakly.*

ERIK

You do know this country is quarantined? What do you think the patrol boats are for?

SPIKE

I know there's a quarantine. But I thought it was only for us.

ERIK

Quarantine is for any poor fucker who puts one toe on this island. Hit land, you never leave.

SPIKE

. . . You can come to my town. After I take my mum to the doctor.

ERIK

Where is this doctor?

They have reached the brow of the next hill.

Just a few miles away now, the smoke from DR KELSON'S *fire rises into the sky.*

SPIKE

There.

ERIK *gazes at the smoke.*

Not far.

ERIK

Not far? You try carrying your mother for a bit.

ERIK *eases* ISLA *off his back.*

Think I'd better take a break.

EXT. COUNTRYSIDE – DAY

ERIK, SPIKE *and* ISLA *sit on grass.*

SPIKE *is using his knife to cut thin slivers from an apple, and feeding them to* ISLA.

She looks dazed. And eats only barely. ERIK *is also eating an apple.*

ERIK

First meal in a day and a half.

SPIKE *gestures at his backpack.*

SPIKE

Have another.

ERIK *looks inside – and sees it is absolutely full of apples.*

ERIK

. . . You seem to really like apples.

ISLA

(*quiet*)

. . . Dad.

SPIKE *looks round at* ISLA.

I'm cold.

SPIKE *pulls his jacket off and arranges it over her shoulders.*

ERIK

. . . Why does she call you 'Dad'? I'm sure there's a lot of inbreeding in these parts, but –

ERIK waves a finger between SPIKE and ISLA.

– this feels unlikely.

SPIKE

She's just confused. She's not like this all the time. Most of the time she's just like she always was.

ISLA's head lifts. With an effort, she focuses her gaze.

ISLA

Who's like she always was?

SPIKE

. . . You, Mum.

ISLA

Oh.

ISLA looks around. Then sees ERIK – as if for the first time.

. . . Who are you?

ERIK

Erik. And this is your father, Spike.

ISLA

What?

SPIKE

He's being silly, Mum.

ISLA

He's being a dick.

SPIKE looks shocked.

SPIKE

Mum!

(*to Erik*)

Sorry.

(*to Isla*)

He saved our lives.

ISLA

I know a dick when I see one.

ISLA *gets to her feet, unsteadily.*

Remind me where we're going, again?

SPIKE

The doctor.

ISLA

. . . Yes.

Beat.

Okay. Let's go.

EXT. FOREST – DAY

Forest. In which the PREGNANT INFECTED *appears.*

She makes a few steps – then is hit by another contraction.

She can't go any further. She props herself up against something in the forest.

The SIDE OF A TRAIN CARRIAGE.

EXT. FOREST – DAY

SPIKE, ISLA *and* ERIK *walk through forest.* ISLA *is slow, but managing.*

ERIK

Why do they get so huge? The *bärsärk*.

SPIKE

Sam says, on some the infection works like steroids. I don't really know what steroids are, but I guess that's why they turn Alpha.

ERIK

Alpha. You make them sound like stockbrokers. *Bärsärk is better.* You know what a *bärsärk* is? Berserker. Crazy Viking warrior.

Beat.

I'm actually a Viking. Maybe if I got infected, I'd turn into a –

AT THAT MOMENT, *there is a soaring* CRY *from near them in the forest. A labour pain.*

SPIKE, ERIK *and* ISLA *all freeze, and their heads flick round to the source of the noise.*

But their expressions are different.

SPIKE *and* ERIK *don't recognise the cry for what it is. To them, it is unearthly and terrifying.*

ISLA *does. She frowns, puzzled. Then she focuses. Her mind snapped back into itself.*

ERIK
(*continued*)

What the fuck was that?

SPIKE

I don't know.

ANOTHER CRY *from the forest.*

We should get out of here.

ERIK

Uh – yeah.

SPIKE *and* ERIK *start moving again.*

It's only after SPIKE *has taken a few steps that he realises –* ISLA *isn't moving with them.*

SPIKE *looks round for her. But she's gone.*

Then he glimpses her. Walking through the trees towards the sound of the cries.

SPIKE

Mum!

SPIKE *starts after her, and* ERIK *grabs his arm.*

ERIK

Where are you going?

SPIKE *yanks himself free.*

SPIKE

I'm not *leaving* her.

CUT TO –

EXT. FOREST/TRAIN CARRIAGES – DAY

– ISLA*, stepping out of undergrowth, to* REVEAL *a train. A line of carriages, sitting on the tracks, in the middle of the forest.*

Abandoned for twenty-eight years, the woods have grown up around it. The windows are semi-opaque with dirt. Dead leaves lie like snowdrifts around it.

In front of ISLA*, a door hangs open.* ANOTHER CRY*. From very close.*

ISLA *steps forward – through the door, into the train –*

– as SPIKE *and* ERIK *appear from the undergrowth behind her.*

SPIKE

Mum! Stop!

INT. TRAIN CARRIAGE – DAY

ISLA *stands in the carriage, and gazes – at the* PREGNANT INFECTED WOMAN.

She's sat on the floor of the train, bracing herself against the seats on either side.

The two lock eyes for a moment. Then the woman's face contorts as another massive contraction hits her.

As she screams out, ISLA *steps forward . . .*

. . . and kneels in front of her.

SPIKE *appears behind* ISLA. *Stunned by what he sees.*

SPIKE

Mum?

He reaches forward, grabs her shoulder.

No, Mum, no – what are you –

ISLA *takes the hands of the* INFECTED WOMAN.

Don't touch her!

The woman's hands clamp around ISLA'S.

No, no –

SPIKE *reaches down to try to pull at* ISLA'S *forearm –*

– and as he does so, the woman lets out another huge cry. And the head of a BABY *starts to appear between her legs. Instinctively,* SPIKE *recoils, pulling back.*

And ISLA *reaches down, and cups the* BABY'S *head.* ERIK *appears behind* SPIKE.

ERIK

Holy . . . Fucking . . . Shit.

THE NEXT MOMENT, *the* INFECTED WOMAN *launches into a final massive push – and the* BABY *is suddenly delivered into* ISLA'S *hands.*

It's a little girl.

Silence – except for the gasping breaths of the INFECTED WOMAN, *who sinks backwards to the floor, and lies still.*

ISLA *looks down at the* BABY. *And the* BABY *– starts crying.*

In its face, and eyes, it shows no sign of infection.

ISLA *smiles. Then, cradling the* BABY *in one arm, she lifts the* UMBILICAL CORD *with her free hand.*

ISLA

Spike. Cut it.

SPIKE *stares.*

Spike. Cut it.

Hands shaking – SPIKE *obeys. He pulls out his lock knife –*

ERIK

. . . No fucking way.

– and cuts the cord.

ISLA

Well done, Spike.

ERIK

You're all insane . . .

SPIKE

Mum . . .

SPIKE *is staring at the* BABY.

. . . She doesn't look infected.

ISLA

She isn't.

AT THAT MOMENT *– the* INFECTED WOMAN *suddenly sits* BOLT UPRIGHT. LOCKED BACK *into the* RAGE STATE.

Her hands snap out to grab ISLA *–*

– then there is an EXPLOSION *of* NOISE.

– ERIK has fired his rifle. He hits the woman in the head. As she falls back down –

– ERIK starts backing away to the exit of the carriage.

ERIK

You guys are crazy – sick fucking crazy English –

He reaches the door.

I'm going on my own. Fuck you, you inbred psychos –

SUDDENLY – ERIK is YANKED with incredible force. Out of SIGHT.

SPIKE immediately knows what just happened.

SPIKE

Mum, get up –

As ISLA rises, holding the BABY –

– we hear ERIK SCREAM.

Then the scream is abruptly CUT SHORT.

SPIKE and ISLA start backing down the carriage as, from outside – we hear the lion-like roar of an ALPHA.

INT. TRAIN CARRIAGE – DAY

Halfway down the next carriage, SPIKE looks back – and sees the ALPHA climb inside. Holding ERIK's head in one hand, with the spine dangling.

SPIKE lifts his bow. Aims, and fires.

The arrow FLIES down the length of the carriages – and embeds in the ALPHA's chest.

And does absolutely nothing. The ALPHA starts to charge.

INT. TRAIN CARRIAGES – DAY

SPIKE and ISLA run the length of the train –

– as the ALPHA *thunders behind them.*

But its massive size is actually an impediment, down the narrow space.

SPIKE *and* ISLA *have reached the last carriage.*

SPIKE *tries to open the door – but foliage is holding it shut.*

He kicks at the door with all his strength.

Just as the ALPHA *reaches their carriage – the door opens. He pushes* ISLA, *still holding the* BABY, *through.*

Then turns and fires another ARROW.

Again, it embeds in the chest. And does nothing.

As the ALPHA *claws its way down the carriage, still holding* ERIK'S *head –*

– SPIKE *slips out, following* ISLA.

EXT. MEADOW – DAY

SPIKE *and* ISLA *run out of the forest, into a* MEADOW.

The far side of the meadow slopes up, to the brow of another hill – beyond which, SMOKE *rises.*

They are so close to their goal.

But moments later, the ALPHA *bursts out of the treeline.* SPIKE *stops. Turns. Lifts his bow.*

SPIKE

Mum – run to the smoke! RUN TO THE SMOKE!

SPIKE *fires an arrow – which hits the* ALPHA *again.*

Keep running, Mum!

He quickly notches another, and fires. And hits again.

With four arrows in it, the ALPHA *keeps running, completely unaffected.*

SPIKE *starts to notch again.*

ISLA
(*calm*)

Spike.

SPIKE *instantly realises* – ISLA *is still with him. She hasn't kept running.*

SPIKE *turns – to see* ISLA *behind him, holding the* BABY. *And beside her – there is a* MAN.

He's in his seventies. He's naked. Bald. No body hair – even eyebrows. And he's painted himself, head to toe, in an ORANGE STAIN. *The colour is deep, and streaked.*

Set in the orange, his eyes seem unusually white, and staring.

In his right hand, he holds what looks like a long, straight stick. But is, in fact, a length of narrow copper pipe.

Painted blue.

The sight is completely bizarre.

BEHIND SPIKE – *the* ALPHA *has almost reached them. Is only ten feet away.*

Then – the MAN *raises the blue length of pipe, and puts it to his lips. And gives a single sharp* BLOW.

Something flies out of the end of the pipe. And embeds into the ALPHA'S *neck.*

VIRTUALLY IMMEDIATELY – *the* ALPHA *reacts.*

Its sprint is suddenly checked – slowing.

First to a run. Then, within another stride, to a walk. Then it stops. Only two feet from SPIKE.

The ALPHA *towers over the small boy. Its eyes go vacant. Its jaw slackens.*

As the twisted rage disappears from its face, we see the human beneath.

A beat, as the ALPHA *stands upright.*

Swaying slightly. Blood running out of the arrow wounds.

MAN

Morphine. And xylazine. Extremely fast-acting.

The MAN *steps past* SPIKE, *towards the* ALPHA.

Excuse my appearance. I paint myself in iodine. It's an excellent prophylactic. The virus doesn't like iodine at all.

The MAN *reaches out, and gently removes* ERIK'S *head from the* ALPHA'S *grip.*

The ALPHA *doesn't resist.*

I think I'll take that, Samson.

The MAN *turns back to* SPIKE.

I call this one Samson. He's lived in the area for a good three years now. I usually keep my distance from him, of course.

SPIKE *is still staring at the* MAN, *trying to process.*

SPIKE

. . . Sir.

MAN

'Sir.' Such good manners.

SPIKE

. . . Are you Doctor Kelson?

A beat. Then KELSON *nods.*

KELSON

Yes. I am.

SPIKE

I'm Spike. This is my mum, Isla. And this is . . . a baby.

Beat.

We need your help.

EXT. MEADOW SLOPE – DAY

SPIKE, ISLA *– holding the* BABY *– and* KELSON *approach the brow of the hill.*

On the other side of the hill, the smoke rises. At the top, they stop. And look down, REVEALING *–*

EXT. THE BONE TEMPLE – DAY

– below them, an extraordinary structure.

It is a kind of massive artwork, in the form of a church-sized building, made entirely of human bones.

The walls are stacked femurs. Layered hip bones fan out as decorative flourishes. Ribcages form lattice-like pillars.

In the centre of the structure, there is a spire, like a slender pyramid, made of a spiral of skulls.

Around the main structure, there are spurs of smaller arrangements – like Buddhist stupas, arranged around the main temple.

And surrounding the stupas there is a ditch, and a skeletal fence, with sharpened bone shards jutting out like barbed wire.

EXT. MEADOW SLOPE – DAY

ISLA *looks down at the structure, cradling the baby.*

She looks gently hypnotised. Unconcerned. Almost calmed, as if experiencing a déjà vu that feels expected, or appropriate.

SPIKE *turns to* KELSON.

SPIKE

. . . What is that?

KELSON smiles.

KELSON

I've been waiting more than thirteen years for someone to ask that question. I often thought I would die here alone, from age or starvation or violence, never having had the chance to reply.

Beat.

Do you know the words 'Memento Mori'?

SPIKE

. . . No.

KELSON

It's Latin. Ironically, a dead language. The words mean – 'Remember Death'.

KELSON glances at the boy.

Remember you must die. It is possibly the most meaningful statement that can be made.

KELSON looks back at the structure.

So I thought it was worth saying properly.

EXT. THE BONE TEMPLE – DAY

SPIKE, ISLA and KELSON walk through the temple area, past the stupas, towards the main structure.

KELSON

There were so many dead. Infected and non-infected alike, because they are alike. Every skull, a set of thoughts. The sockets saw. The jaws spoke and swallowed.

SPIKE touches one of the stupas –

– and from the sides, a few finger bones dislodge and tinkle to the grass.

SPIKE

Oh – I'm sorry –

KELSON

No, don't worry. It's not precious, in that way. Things made of bones collapse. Time, the elements, or Spike's hand – the Memento Mori is actualised.

DR KELSON *holds up* ERIK'S *head.*

Did you know this man?

SPIKE

He was called Erik. He saved our lives.

KELSON *nods.*

KELSON

Good for him. Let's find Erik his home.

EXT. THE BONE TEMPLE/FIRE – DAY

The structure is built by a stream – which runs through the temple grounds.

By the stream, a wood fire burns – with a large stack of chopped wood beside.

And over the fire, there is a domestic pressurised water cylinder, suspended on chains. The flames have blackened the metal and scorched off the paint.

And a section of the cylinder has been cut out, to create a hatch that can be locked back in place with clamps.

SPIKE *watches, as* KELSON *opens the hatch, releasing a jet of pressurised steam.*

Then he puts ERIK'S *head inside, using a long* PITCHFORK. *And locks back the hatch.*

EXT. THE BONE TEMPLE/MAIN STRUCTURE – SUNSET

A little distance away, ISLA *sits in the main structure, holding the sleeping* BABY *in her arms.*

EXT. THE BONE TEMPLE/FIRE – SUNSET

The SUN *lowers in the sky, nearing the horizon line – as* KELSON *unlocks the hatch. And removes* ERIK'S *head with the trident.*

It is an unrecognisable shape – a mass of bursting whitish flesh and hair.

KELSON *places the head in the stream. In the running water, the flesh falls easily away. Leaving the skull.*

KELSON *removes the* SKULL, *and looks at it. Turns it over in his hand.*

KELSON

Alas, poor Erik.

Then hands it to SPIKE.

Choose a place for him.

EXT. THE BONE TEMPLE – SUNSET

SPIKE *walks through the temple, holding the* SKULL.

He chooses a spot on one of the stupas – and rests it there.

KELSON

Very nice. Well done, Spike.

Beat.

The baby is newborn.

SPIKE

It was from an infected.

KELSON

How interesting. The magic of the placenta. I had wondered if that might happen.

Beat.

Is that why you came to find me? The baby?

SPIKE

. . . No.

INT. THE BONE TEMPLE/MAIN STRUCTURE – NIGHT

The main structure is a partial dome – with no roof.

In the middle of the structure is the base of the tall spire of skulls.

Night has fallen.

The area is lit by the sawn top-half of skulls.

Inside the skulls is tallow – rendered human fat, from which a length of material burns slowly. Like candles.

SPIKE *holds the* BABY, *watching – as* KELSON *examines* ISLA. *They look as if they are performing a strange ritual.*

KELSON *holds his fingers in a shape – forming a triangle, between forefingers and thumbs; interlacing the first two fingers of each hand.*

And ISLA *tries to replicate. Slowly. Uncertainly.*

Then DR KELSON *reaches out and touches under her chin, gently, at different points around her neck.*

KELSON

Isla – it would be very helpful to check your breasts, and under your arms. Is that okay?

ISLA *nods.*

DR KELSON *reaches under* ISLA'S *shirt.*

Is that tender? Right there?

ISLA *shakes her head.*

What about here?

ISLA

No.

KELSON *removes his hands.*

KELSON

Your feelings of confusion. Do they feel like episodes? Phases? Or does it feel more constant?

ISLA

It was waves. But – now –

ISLA *hesitates.*

I think the tide is coming in.

KELSON

I asked you to remember a word.

ISLA

Yes.

KELSON

What was it?

ISLA *smiles.*

ISLA

Was it –

She pauses.

Then she shakes her head.

KELSON *takes* ISLA*'s hand.*

KELSON

Let's sit.

He leads her to SPIKE*, and they sit in a small circle, in the glow from the tallow candles.*

SPIKE and ISLA wait for KELSON.

KELSON chooses his words. Then speaks.

Isla. I have no diagnostic equipment, and I can't take a biopsy. But from what I can observe, I think you have cancer. It may have spread from your brain to your body, or your body to your brain. Either way, it has metastasised. It explains your symptoms, and – I'm afraid – the masses on your breasts and lymph nodes. I'm very sorry.

ISLA has been looking away, as KELSON speaks.

ISLA

When I'm confused, I know I'm confused. I feel surprised at myself, as I say strange things. But I say them anyway.

Beat.

Not all of me is confused. I know I have cancer.

ISLA looks at SPIKE.

I didn't know how to tell you, Spike. I was too scared. I needed someone else to tell you, but – no one did.

SPIKE looks from ISLA to KELSON.

SPIKE

I don't understand. Are you saying you can't make Mum better?

KELSON

I wish I could. But it's not possible.

SPIKE

What does that mean? Is she going to die? Will the cancer kill her?

KELSON

Yes.

SPIKE

. . . When?

KELSON

It's hard to say. Soon.

SPIKE

Will it hurt?

ISLA

Spikey, my love – it already hurts.

SPIKE

No. *No*. This can't be –

(*breaks off*)

Doctor – you *must* be able to help her. You need a medicine. One of the *old* medicines. If you tell me where a hospital was, I can go there. Tell me, and I'll bring the medicine back.

KELSON

There is no medicine that can cure her, Spike.

SPIKE

Please. You must be able to help us. I'm *asking* you to please help us.

ISLA

Spike.

SPIKE

No – *please*.

KELSON *looks at* SPIKE. *Unreadable. The tallow lamps flicker.*

Doctor Kelson. I'm begging you.

SPIKE *starts crying.*

It was so hard to get here. So hard to find you.

ISLA

Spike.

SPIKE *is sobbing.*

Spike, come here.

ISLA opens her arms.

Come.

SPIKE moves to ISLA.

She folds SPIKE and the BABY up in her arms.

I'm sorry. I should have told you. I should have told you.

As they sit together, REVEAL –

– that KELSON has gone.

Where he sat, the space is empty. SPIKE, ISLA and the BABY are alone.

Beats pass, as ISLA strokes SPIKE's head, and the boy cries quietly.

Around them, the skulls of the main structure are illuminated in the orange flame of the lamps.

As if the massed souls of the temple are watching. Then – ISLA looks up.

KELSON is standing a few feet away. Half in darkness. Holding the blue blowgun.

ISLA and KELSON lock eyes. Held. For a long beat.

Then –

– ISLA nods.

ISLA
(*continued; soft*)

Spike.

SPIKE is buried in ISLA's hug.

SPIKE

Yes.

ISLA

The doctor can't make me better. But . . . he can help me.

SPIKE sits up. Looks at ISLA.

SPIKE

I don't understand.

ISLA kisses him.

ISLA

I do. I want you to try to always remember that. I do understand.

SPIKE

But –

SPIKE stiffens –

– as a DART hits his back. Then – SPIKE relaxes.

The BABY rests in the crook of his arm. A moment later – a DART hits ISLA.

She stiffens. Then relaxes.

In SPIKE's arms, the BABY starts crying.

But the sound is distant, and almost musical. KELSON appears beside them.

KELSON

Spike.

Slowly, dreamily, SPIKE looks up at KELSON.

Memento Mori. What did it mean?

SPIKE

. . . Remember we must die.

KELSON

And it is true. But there are many kinds of death, and some are better than others.

KELSON kneels beside them.

The best are peaceful. Where we leave each other in love.

Beat.

You love your mother.

SPIKE

I love her.

KELSON

And Isla, you love Spike.

ISLA

So much.

KELSON

Memento Amoris.

KELSON reaches out. Takes ISLA's hand.

They stand. And walk into the shadows, leaving SPIKE and the BABY alone.

The BABY stops crying.

The tallow lamps flicker. The flames light the watching skulls.

The spire of skulls reaches into the sky, where a carpet of stars shines.

SPIKE gazes into the walls of the main structure.

CUT TO –

EXT. THE BONE TEMPLE – NIGHT

– ISLA. She is standing in the bone temple. Chin raised. Looking up at the stars. Smiling slightly.

Half a beat later – she is decapitated.

She drops – revealing DR KELSON behind her with a MACHETE.

EXT. THE BONE TEMPLE/MAIN STRUCTURE – NIGHT

SPIKE sits with the BABY.

Dream beats.

Time, with no measurement, passes.

Then – KELSON *reappears. Holding a* SKULL*. Kelson sits beside* SPIKE.

He gently takes the baby from SPIKE*'s arms. And replaces the* BABY *with the* SKULL.

KELSON

Spike.

SPIKE *looks at* KELSON.

Find a place for her. The best one of all.

Beat. Then SPIKE *looks up –*

– at the spire, and the stars.

EXT. THE BONE TEMPLE/SKULL SPIRE – NIGHT

SPIKE *climbs the skull walls of the spire.*

The moonlit landscape of England starts to reveal itself around him.

He climbs, until he reaches the very top. There, he places ISLA*'s skull.*

Then remains. Holding on to the sides.

EXT. LANDSCAPE – DAY

DAYLIGHT.

In the massive landscape – the tiny figure of SPIKE *and his backpack.*

EXT. CAUSEWAY – DAY

The causeway.

Across it, Holy Island.

And the GATE.

High tide is reaching the point where water suddenly spills over the road.

Covering it.

EXT. CAUSEWAY/GATE – DAY

JAMIE *is sleeping on one of the* LOOKOUT TOWERS, *either side of the gate.*

He looks gaunt. Shattered. JENNY *climbs the ladder to him.* ANTHONY *waits below.*

When JENNY *sees him, she puts a hand on* JAMIE'S *shoulder. He wakes with a start.*

JAMIE

I fell asleep – fuck –

JENNY

You needed to sleep.

JAMIE

Did anyone –

JENNY

No.

JAMIE *grabs* JENNY'S *wrist.*

JAMIE

Please, Jenny. Let me go out after them.

JENNY

I'm sorry, Jamie. If I make an exception for you, what do I do the next time this happens?

JAMIE

But –

JAMIE *is* INTERRUPTED –

– by the sound of a BABY, *crying.* JAMIE *cuts off.*

Stares at JENNY.

Who looks equally confused.

EXT. CAUSEWAY/GATE – DAY

ANTHONY *pulls the gate open, and* JAMIE *and* JENNY *exit –*

– to REVEAL, *sitting a few feet away,* SPIKE'S BACKPACK.

And, swaddled in the back, head poking out of the top, is the BABY.

JENNY

. . . What the hell?

JAMIE

That's Spike's bag.

As JENNY *reaches down to pick the* BABY *up –*

– JAMIE *runs forward.*

He shouts across the causeway.

SPIKE!

No reply. No one visible in the distance.

SPIKE!

The sea swallows up his voice.

SPIKE!

CUT TO –

EXT. ROAD – DAY

– SPIKE.

Cooking a skinned rabbit over a fire.

TITLE:

SPIKE is sitting on the verge of an overgrown road, strewn with rusted vehicles.

Beside the road, a line of ELECTRICITY PYLONS stretches off into the green landscape.

Over the years, they have been overgrown with IVY. They look like vast trees.

As SPIKE gazes at the flames –

– he hears the sound of quick movement, nearby.

CUT TO –

– three INFECTED.

Moving fast along the road, towards him.

CUT TO –

SPIKE's face. He's calm.

His bow is pulled back. He's waiting.

Aiming.

Then – releasing.

CUT TO –

– an INFECTED being shot in the NECK.

As it falls, we see there are two more, running behind. Towards SPIKE.

Almost immediately –

– the next falls. Also hit in the neck.

CUT TO –

– SPIKE drawing an arrow on the last INFECTED.

He waits – tracking the tip of the arrow with the INFECTED'S HEAD as it sprints towards him.

The INFECTED is getting frighteningly close –

– but SPIKE doesn't flinch.

He waits until what feels the last moment. Then releases.

The arrow flies STRAIGHT into the INFECTED'S mouth. The tip lances out through the back of its neck.

And it drops. Flat on its face.

MAN

That was nice.

SPIKE *whirls –*

– to see a MAN standing on the road behind him. Just a few feet away.

The MAN is thirty-eight. When he speaks, it is with a Scottish accent.

He has striking shoulder-length blond hair.

His fingers are clustered in gold sovereign rings, as if to act like knuckledusters. He has gold- and silver-chain bracelets. And he wears a tracksuit. It looks almost box-fresh.

On his head, there is a tiara. Around his neck, there's a necklace.

It holds a GOLD CRUCIFIX. It hangs upside down. SPIKE stares at the MAN.

MAN

(*continued*)

You handled yourself well, young man. I saw the whole thing.

AT THAT MOMENT –

– figures start to emerge from all around SPIKE. *Rising from the tall grasses by the side of the road. Seven of them.*

All young, in their late teens and early twenties. Two female. Five male.

They also wear jewellery and tracksuits – though their clothes are clearly much repaired: a patchwork construction, from other tracksuits.

And they all have shoulder-length blonde hair – but theirs is dyed. Roots showing to various degrees.

Then the MAN *smiles.*

In contrast to the rest of his appearance – which is oddly immaculate for this world –

– his teeth are yellow. Never cleaned. Some are brown, and dying. One is missing.

MAN
(*continued*)
My name's Jimmy. Let's be friends.

END.